FUN FACT FILE: NORTH AMERICAN ANIMALS

20 FUN FACTS ABOUT MONARCH BUTTERFLIES

BY VANESSA OSWALD

Gareth Stevens PUBLISHING

Please visit our website, www.garethstevens.com. For a free color catalog of all our high-quality books, call toll free 1-800-542-2595 or fax 1-877-542-2596.

Library of Congress Cataloging-in-Publication Data

Names: Oswald, Vanessa, author.
Title: 20 fun facts about monarch butterflies / Vanessa Oswald.
Other titles: Twenty fun facts about monarch butterflies
Description: New York : Gareth Stevens Publishing, [2021] | Series: Fun fact file : North American animals | Includes index.
Identifiers: LCCN 2019050727 | ISBN 9781538257685 (library binding) | ISBN 9781538257661 (paperback) | ISBN 9781538257678 | ISBN 9781538257692 (ebook)
Subjects: LCSH: Monarch butterfly–Juvenile literature.
Classification: LCC QL561.D3 O89 2021 | DDC 595.78/9–dc23
LC record available at https://lccn.loc.gov/2019050727

First Edition

Published in 2021 by
Gareth Stevens Publishing
111 East 14th Street, Suite 349
New York, NY 10003

Designer: Sarah Liddell
Editor: Kate Mikoley

Photo credits: Cover, p. 1 (main) New_Nature_Photography/Shutterstock.com; file folder used throughout David Smart/Shutterstock.com; binder clip used throughout luckyraccoon/Shutterstock.com; wood grain background used throughout ARENA Creative/Shutterstock.com; p. 5 Brian Lasenby/Shutterstock.com; p. 6 (monarch) Darkdiamond67/Shutterstock.com; pp. 6 (viceroy), 19 Sari ONeal/Shutterstock.com; p. 7 File Upload Bot (Magnus Manske)/Shutterstock.com; p. 8 © iStockphoto.com/BirdImages; p. 9 Sean Xu/Shutterstock.com; p. 10 Steven Russell Smith Ohio/Shutterstock.com; p. 11 CHAINFOTO24/Shutterstock.com; p. 12 Sylvain CORDIER/Contributor/Gammo-Rapho/Getty Images; p. 13 (butterfly) Butterfly Hunter/Shutterstock.com; p. 13 (map) kateukraine/Shutterstock.com; p. 14 (female) Stefan Mokrzecki/Shutterstock.com; p. 14 (male) Steven Russell Smith Ohio/Shutterstock.com; p. 15 ParkerDeen/E+/Getty Images; p. 16 Nicolas Primola/Shutterstock.com; p. 17 Cathy Keifer/Shutterstock.com; p. 18 Elliotte Rusty Harold/Shutterstock.com; p. 20 del Monaco/Shutterstock.com; p. 21 Sue Felix/Shutterstock.com; p. 22 Raging Bull Photography/Shutterstock.com; p. 23 PEDRO PARDO/Staff/AFP/Getty Images; p. 24 Paul Reeves Photography/Shutterstock.com; p. 25 Robin T. Cowen/Shutterstock.com; p. 26 Steven Russell Smith Ohio/Shutterstock.com; p. 27 JHVEphoto/Shutterstock.com; p. 29 iyd39/Shutterstock.com.

Printed in the United States of America

CPSIA compliance information: Batch #CS20GS: For further information contact Gareth Stevens, New York, New York at 1-800-542-2595.

CONTENTS

Words in the glossary appear in **bold** type the first time they are used in the text.

THE MOST POPULAR BUTTERFLY

Monarch butterflies are flying **insects** that can be **identified** by their bright orange wings with black markings. This striking coloring makes them one of the most well-known butterflies.

Like all butterflies, monarch butterflies go through metamorphosis, a series of changes from an egg to an adult butterfly. They're also known for their long **migrations**. These butterflies travel far and see many parts of the United States, Canada, and Mexico. Read on to find out more about these cool creatures!

An adult monarch butterfly has an orange, black, and white pattern—but these insects start out as white or yellow eggs.

WATCH THE WINGS!

FUN FACT: 1

YOU CAN TELL IF A BUTTERFLY IS A MONARCH BY LOOKING AT ITS WINGS.

Monarchs look similar to other butterflies called viceroys. Both have orange wings filled with thin black lines called veins, and a black border. Viceroys have a black line crossing their back wings. Monarchs don't.

Monarch butterflies also have two rows of white spots on the border of their wings.

Monarch butterflies don't taste good to most predators. Their colorful wings let the predators know this.

FUN FACT: 2

A MONARCH BUTTERFLY'S COLORING ACTS AS A WARNING.

As caterpillars, monarch butterflies eat and store food from a toxic plant called milkweed. This makes them poisonous to predators. The butterflies' colors warn predators not to eat them.

The black-headed grosbeak, shown here, is a common predator of the monarch butterfly in the winter. They can eat the insects without being poisoned.

FUN FACT: 3

ANIMALS STILL EAT MONARCH BUTTERFLIES EVEN THOUGH THEY'RE POISONOUS!

Most of the time, an animal that eats a monarch butterfly won't die. It will just get sick and learn not to eat one again. Still, some predators aren't affected by the poison at all.

BUILDING A BUTTERFLY

FUN FACT: 4

THE MONARCH BUTTERFLY HAS SPECIAL PARTS IT USES TO DRINK AND SMELL.

Monarch butterflies use their proboscis like a straw to sip nectar from plants.

Butterflies have a head, **thorax**, and **abdomen**. The head includes the eyes, two antennae, two palpi, and a proboscis. The antennae and palpi help it smell. The proboscis helps it drink.

THE BUTTERFLY BODY

All insects have the same three basic body parts: a head, thorax, and abdomen.

FUN FACT: 5

A MONARCH BUTTERFLY HAS SIX LEGS, BUT IT SOMETIMES LOOKS LIKE IT ONLY HAS FOUR!

Monarch butterflies have four wings: two hindwings and two forewings.

The monarch butterfly's legs and wings are attached to its thorax. The two front legs are small and close to the thorax, making them hard to see.

LONG-DISTANCE TRAVELERS

FUN FACT: 6

SOME BUTTERFLIES TRAVEL NEARLY 3,000 MILES (4,828 KM) DURING THEIR MIGRATION JOURNEY.

Monarchs often fly south to Mexico or California in the fall. This takes up to two months. The butterflies travel 50 to 100 miles (80.5 to 161 km) a day!

While traveling, monarch butterflies stay in groups, called roosts, at night.

MONARCH MIGRATIONS

The migration back north happens in spring. The trip happens in stages, with each of four **generations** traveling some of the way. The last generation flies south again the next fall. This generation lives the longest.

BUTTERFLY BREEDING

FUN FACT: 7

YOU CAN TELL IF A MONARCH IS MALE OR FEMALE BY ITS WINGS.

Female monarch butterflies are often darker in color than males. Males have two black spots on their hindwings. Females don't. If you see these spots, the butterfly is male.

Female monarch butterflies also have thicker black wing veins than males.

Monarch butterflies lay their eggs on a milkweed plant. They lay one egg at a time—and often only one per leaf!

FUN FACT: 8

FEMALE MONARCH BUTTERFLIES LAY 300 TO 500 EGGS IN 2 TO 5 WEEKS!

Male and female monarch butterflies come out of **hibernation** in February and March. They migrate north to find a place for the female to lay the eggs.

METAMORPHOSIS

FUN FACT: 9

BUTTERFLIES DON'T START THEIR LIVES AS BUTTERFLIES!

There are four stages in the monarch life cycle. First is the egg. Next, the egg becomes a larva (caterpillar), which becomes a pupa (chrysalis), and finally an adult butterfly. This process of change is called metamorphosis.

Monarchs are in their egg for about 4 days. They are larvae for about 14 days and pupae for 8 to 15 days before becoming adult butterflies.

The caterpillar will finish eating its shell even after it's made enough room to get out!

FUN FACT: 10

MONARCH CATERPILLARS EAT THEIR OWN EGGSHELLS.

About four days after a monarch butterfly lays an egg on a milkweed plant, a caterpillar hatches, or comes out. The caterpillar eats its eggshell to get out. It may also eat other eggs once it's out.

LIFE OF A CATERPILLAR

FUN FACT: 11

MONARCH CATERPILLARS DON'T EAT ANYTHING BESIDES MILKWEED PLANTS.

The plants provide enough food for these tiny creatures. Monarch caterpillars eat so much milkweed after they're born that they grow almost 3,000 times their size in just 10 to 15 days!

Monarch caterpillars have yellow, black, and white stripes.

Molting gives caterpillars room to grow. They eat their exoskeleton after shedding it!

FUN FACT: 12

MONARCH CATERPILLARS GET RID OF THEIR SKIN!

A monarch caterpillar molts, or sheds, its **exoskeleton**, five times before it's ready to form its chrysalis. It will reach about 2 inches (5 cm) long after its final molt.

MAKING A CHRYSALIS

FUN FACT: 13

MONARCH CATERPILLARS OFTEN LEAVE THEIR MILKWEED PLANTS TO BECOME PUPAE.

Before making their chrysalis, they make a silk pad on the bottom of a branch or leaf. They hook to this pad, and then they shed their last skin and form their chrysalis.

The monarch stays upside down in the chrysalis until it's ready to break out as a butterfly.

Monarchs are often a little wet when they come out of the chrysalis. Their wings have to dry off before they can fly.

FUN FACT: 14

THE CHRYSALIS CHANGES COLOR.

First, it's green with gold dots. Then it becomes white, and finally, see-through. A monarch caterpillar stays in its chrysalis for around 9 to 15 days before emerging, or coming out, as a butterfly.

AMAZING ADULT BUTTERFLIES

FUN FACT: 15

MONARCH BUTTERFLIES WEIGH LESS THAN A PAPER CLIP!

A full-grown monarch butterfly's wingspan can reach close to 5 inches (13 cm). They only weigh 0.0095 to 0.026 ounces (0.27 to 0.74 g).

Butterfly wings are very light. They're made of a kind of matter called chitin.

The word "monarch" means a ruler, such as a king or a queen. Some people call the monarch butterfly the "king of butterflies."

FUN FACT: 16

THE MONARCH BUTTERFLY'S SCIENTIFIC NAME, *DANAUS PLEXIPPUS*, MEANS "SLEEPY TRANSFORMATION" IN GREEK.

Inside the chrysalis, the pupa breathes through little tubes. The body may look at rest, but a lot of change is happening as the pupa becomes a butterfly.

DINING WITH BUTTERFLIES

FUN FACT: 17

MONARCH BUTTERFLIES DRINK THEIR FOOD!

Monarch butterflies are herbivores, meaning they only eat plants. They drink nectar from flowers and water using their proboscis. When monarch butterflies are not using their proboscis, they curl it up.

Monarch butterflies generally drink nectar from brightly colored flowers.

Goldenrod is one of the most common plants monarch butterflies drink nectar from. These plants have clusters, or groups, of many small flowers.

FUN FACT: 18

BUTTERFLIES TASTE WITH THEIR FEET!

They have special sensors that allow them to taste a plant when they land on it. Unlike bees, which also drink nectar from flowers, butterflies do not move much pollen from plant to plant.

DEALING WITH DANGERS

FUN FACT: 19

A MONARCH BUTTERFLY CAN'T FLY IF IT'S TOO COLD.

If its body temperature is below 86°F (30°C), a monarch butterfly won't be able to fly. It may sit in a sunny area or move its wings around until it warms up enough.

In the summer, monarch butterflies only live about 2 to 6 weeks. Monarchs that migrate often live through the winter and can live for 6 to 9 months.

Monarch butterflies sometimes gather together in trees to stay warm!

FUN FACT: 20

HABITAT LOSS AND CLIMATE CHANGE ARE PUTTING MONARCH BUTTERFLIES IN DANGER.

Higher levels of a gas called carbon dioxide seem to be making milkweed too toxic for caterpillars. Rising summer temperatures also mean monarchs have to travel farther north to have babies.

JOY OF THE MONARCHS

There are about 17,500 species, or kinds, of butterflies in the world, but monarch butterflies' long journeys and striking colors make them stand out from the rest.

You may be able to see a monarch butterfly in your backyard or at a park. If you see one, you shouldn't touch it. Touching it could hurt its wings. You can also visit a butterfly conservatory—a building where many kinds of butterflies are kept and people can go to observe and learn more about them.

At a conservatory, a butterfly may land on you! This is a great way to see one up close, but be gentle. You shouldn't touch other parts of the butterfly besides the part that's touching you.

GLOSSARY

abdomen: the part of an insect's body that contains the stomach

climate change: long-term change in Earth's climate, caused partly by human activities such as burning oil and natural gas

exoskeleton: the hard outer covering of an animal's body

generation: a group of animals born around the same time

habitat: the natural place where an animal or plant lives

hibernation: the act of passing the winter in a resting state

identify: to find out the name or features of something

insect: a small, often winged, animal with six legs and three main body parts

migration: movement to warmer or colder places for a season

thorax: the middle part of an insect's body. The wings and legs connect to it.

transformation: a change in form or appearance

FOR MORE INFORMATION

BOOKS

Almasy, Kip. *How Do Monarch Butterflies Find Their Way Home?* New York, NY: PowerKids Press, 2018.

Fishman, Jon M. *The Monarch Butterfly's Journey*. Minneapolis, MN: Lerner Publications, 2018.

Hansen, Grace. *Monarch Butterfly Migration*. Minneapolis, MN: Abdo Kids, 2018.

WEBSITES

Butterflies and Moths
www.dkfindout.com/us/animals-and-nature/insects/butterflies-and-moths
Find out about all kinds of butterflies and moths here.

Monarch Butterfly
kids.nationalgeographic.com/animals/invertebrates/insects/monarch-butterfly/
This site includes cool facts about monarch butterflies and their migration patterns.

Monarch Butterfly Metamorphosis
thekidshouldseethis.com/post/monarch-butterfly-metamorphosis-in-hd-the-monarch-manifesto
Watch a video showing the metamorphosis of a caterpillar turning into a butterfly.

INDEX